Blast Off to Reading!®

Student Workbook

by Cheryl Orlassino

Blast Off to Learning

For the web-app for this program, go to

www.BlastOffToReading.com

For the Lesson Slides and other information, go to

www.BlastOffToLearning.com

Published By Blast Off to Learning, LLC
New York

e-mail all inquiries to

contact@BlastOffToLearning.com

ISBN: 9798844215520 - REV E

Exercise 1.1
Write the first letter for the words that identifies the pictures.

1.  _____

2. _____

3. _____

4. _____

5. _____

6. _____

7. _____

8. _____

9. _____

10. _____

11. _____

12. _____

13. _____

14. _____

15. _____

16. _____

17. _____

18. _____

19. _____

Exercise 1.2
Below is the alphabet. Circle the vowels.

a b c d e f g h i j k l m
n o p q r s t u v w x y z

Exercise 1.3
Draw lines to match the first sound of the pictures to the letters.

1.   a

2.   e

3.   i

4.   o

5.   u

Exercise 1.4

Circle the vowel that goes with the beginning sound for each picture below.

1. a   e   i   o   u

2. a   e   i   o   u

3. a   e   i   o   u

4. a   e   i   o   u

Exercise 1.5

Write the vowel that goes with the pictures below.

1.  ☐   4. ☐

2.  ☐   5. ☐

3. ☐

Exercise 2.1
Circle the sound to complete the words.

1.		p_ _	an	in	un
2.		t_ _	ob	ab	ub
3.		b_ _	at	it	ot
4.		f_ _	ax	ix	ox

Exercise 2.2
For each line, circle the word that has a **short** vowel

1.

2.

3.

4.

Exercise 2.3
Circle the sound to complete the words.

1. n_ _	et	it	ot
2. r_ _	og	ag	ug
3. h_ _	an	in	en
4. m_ _	in	an	on

Exercise 2.4
Read the sentences below to your student using the word "blank" for the underlined word choices. Then have him/her choose and circle the correct words for each sentence.

1. <u>My / Me</u> dog likes to go for a walk.

2. They <u>has / have</u> a black cat.

3. What <u>was / does</u> she looking at?

4. Why <u>does / do</u> they want to go there?

5. She <u>does / said</u> that she likes chocolate.

Exercise 2.5

Read the sentences below to your student using the word "blank" for the underlined word choices. Then have him/her choose and circle the correct words for each sentence.

1. Where are <u>he / you</u> going?

2. Where <u>does / do</u> he live?

3. <u>She / He</u> likes her pink dress.

4. <u>What / Who</u> told you to go?

5. We will <u>go / have</u> home later.

6. <u>What / Where</u> are his shoes?

7. Where are <u>you / your</u> books?

Exercise 3.1
Circle the **middle short vowel** sounds for the pictures below.

1. a   e   i   o   u

2. a   e   i   o   u

3. a   e   i   o   u

4. a   e   i   o   u

5. a   e   i   o   u

6. a   e   i   o   u

Exercise 3.2
Fill in the missing short vowels for the words below.

1. 10   t___n

2. v___n

3. b___x

4. m___p

5. s___n

6. p___g

Exercise 3.3

Read the following sentences to your student INCLUDING the words in question. Then have him/her choose and circle the correct spelling for the underlined words.

1. What <u>wuz / was</u> the show about?

2. She <u>has / haz</u> a small house.

3. <u>They / Thay</u> are going out to dinner.

4. <u>Whut / What</u> are you eating?

5. Where <u>duz / does</u> he go after school?

Exercise 3.4

Circle the **middle short vowel** sound for the pictures below.

1.   a   e   i   o   u

2.   a   e   i   o   u

3.   a   e   i   o   u

4.   a   e   i   o   u

5.   a   e   i   o   u

6.   a   e   i   o   u

Exercise 3.5
Fill in the missing letters ('b', 'd' or 'p') for the words below.

1.  __ en

2.  __ at

3.  __ug

4.  li__

5.  __un

6.  mo__

7.  __ an

8.  tu__

9. __in

10. __og

Exercise 3.6
Read the sentences to your student, inserting the word "blank" for the underlined words, and have him/her circle the words to complete the sentences.

1. Where did <u>we / my</u> dog go?

2. <u>They / She</u> have been waiting in line a long time.

3. He <u>have / has</u> a baseball game tonight.

4. My sister <u>was / does</u> not like spiders.

5. He <u>was / is</u> at my house yesterday.

Exercise 3.7
Circle the **middle short vowel** sound for the pictures below.

1.    a   e   i   o   u

2.   a   e   i   o   u

3.   a   e   i   o   u

4.   a   e   i   o   u

Exercise 3.8
Fill in the missing letters for the words below.

1.   m__n

2.   r__g

3.   n__t

4.   h__g

5.   h__n

6.   f__x

7.   c__n

8.   h__t

Exercise 3.9
Read the sentences and circle the matching pictures.

1. The bug is in the tub.

2. My cat is on the rug.

3. The dog is in the box.

4. The lid is on the pot.

5. Get rid of the fat rat.

6. The pig is in the mud.

7. We had a lot of fun.

Exercise 4.1
Review: Fill in the blanks to complete the words.

1.   p __ __

2.   c __ __

3.   b __ __

4.   f __ __

Exercise 4.2
Write the consonant blends for the <u>beginning</u> sounds for the pictures below.

1.   s t __ __

2.   __ __

3.   __ __

4.   __ __ __

5.   __ __ __

6.   __ __

7.   __ __ __

8.   __ __

9.   __ __ __

10.   __ __ __

Exercise 4.3

Write the consonant blends for the <u>ending</u> sounds for the pictures below.

1. stu __ __

2.  te __ __

3. li __ __

4. la __ __

5. pla __ __

6. hu __ __

7. mi __ __

8. be __ __

Exercise 4.4

Circle the letters that make real words (there is one per line).

1. tw _?_   ig   an   on

2. sw _?_   ut   id   im

3. pl _?_   ug   at   in

4. tr _?_   in   ip   ut

5. gr _?_   in   at   ib

Exercise 4.5
Circle the words that make sense in the sentences.

1. Put the list on my <u>desk / milk</u>.

2. You must ask for <u>held / help</u> when you go.

3. I have a lot of milk in my <u>salt / cup</u>.

4. If you want to go, you must <u>ask / last</u> .

5. The twin can swim <u>calm / fast</u>.

6. He <u>went / held</u> on to the flag.

Exercise 5.1
Circle the sound that completes the word.

1. h_____   atch   etch   itch   otch   utch

2.  cr_____   atch   etch   itch   otch   utch

3. sw_____   atch   etch   itch   otch   utch

4. 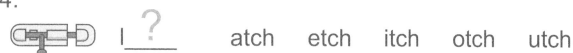 l_____   atch   etch   itch   otch   utch

5. scr_____   atch   etch   itch   otch   utch

Exercise 5.2
Complete the words below.

1. ch___ ___

2. ch___ ___

3. ch___ ___ ___

4. ri___ ___

5. ___ ___ itch

6. p___ ___ ___ ___

Exercise 5.3
Circle the sound to make a real word.

1. sk _?_   itch   etch

2. b _?_   atch   etch

3. cl _?_   itch   utch

4. n _?_   utch   otch

5. sn _?_   atch   utch

6. f _?_   utch   etch

Exercise 5.4
Circle the sounds to make real words (there is only one per line).

1. l __?__   osh   ash   itch

2. cr __?__   ash   itch   ish

3. br __?__   etch   ish   ush

4. st __?__   otch   ush   ash

5. h __?__   esh   ush   etch

Exercise 5.5
Choose 'ch' or 'sh' to make real words.

ch   sh

1. cra_____   4. ca_____   7. _____amp

2. _____ut   5. ra_____   8. ba_____

3. _____at   6. pun_____   9. su_____

Exercise 6.1

Read the sentences to your student and have him/her complete the words with the sounds listed.

ash   atch   ush   ish   ath   itch

1. Make a ___w_____ on a shooting star.

2. Another name for a tattletale is ___sn_____ .

3. If your skin is red and itchy, you may have a ___r_____ .

4. If you go for a walk in the woods, it is best to stay on the ___p_____ .

5. The dog tried to ___sn_____ the bacon from the table.

6. You can ___fl_____ a toilet.

Exercise 6.2

Circle a sound to make a real word (there is one per line).

1. pa_?_	th	sh	ch
2. fl_?_	itch	ash	ish
3. sl_?_	otch	ish	ash
4. ch_?_	on	an	in
5. th_?_	am	in	ish

Exercise 6.3
Complete the words below.

1. l__ __ __

2. p __ __ __ __ __

3. $2+2=4$ m__ __ __

4. sw__ __ __ __

5.  p__ __ __

6. f__ __ __

7. b__ __ __

8. br __ __ __

9. br __ __ __   m__ __ __ __

10.  cr__ __ __

Exercise 6.4
Read the sentences and circle the words that make sense.

1. <u>Of / He</u> has a pet cat.

2. The man sat on top <u>was / of</u> the box.

3. <u>He / The</u> trap had a latch on the top.

4. <u>My / Me</u> leg had a cramp.

5. <u>Of / Was</u> it hot at camp?

6. Do <u>he / you</u> have a pet fish?

Exercise 6.5

Read each sentence to your student, and have him/her write the missing word.

1. A bird lays eggs in a ___ ___ ___ ___.

2. The opposite of fat is ___ ___ ___ ___.

3. If you don't know where you are, you are

   ___ ___ ___ ___.

4. When you add and subtract, you are doing

   ___ ___ ___ ___.

5. When you blow out birthday candles, you make a

   ___ ___ ___ ___.

6. If you are dirty, you should take a ___ ___ ___ ___.

Exercise 6.6

Circle a sound to make a real word.

1. bla_?__	th	sh	st
2. __?_ap	sh	th	sl
3. fa_?__	st	sh	mp
4. __?_ip	th	tr	st
5. __?_at	sh	th	tr

The /nk/ Sounds

Exercise 7.1
Circle the sounds to make real words (there is one per line).

1. dr _?_   ig   ash   ip

2. dr _?_   ank   onk   ish

3. dr _?_   ash   ig   op

4. dr _?_   in   ag   itch

5. dr _?_   am   ink   og

Exercise 7.2
Read the words and circle the answers to the question:

Is the vowel sound in the word **long** or **short**?

1. n<u>e</u>st   long   short

2. m<u>e</u>   long   short

3. l<u>a</u>tch   long   short

4. b<u>a</u>nk   long   short

5. w<u>e</u>   long   short

6. b<u>e</u>   long   short

Exercise 7.3
Read each sentence and circle the words that make sense.

1. She have / has to thank you.

2. He does / was not want to crash the bus.

3. We have / has to go to the bank to get cash.

4. I can not think of / is what to do next.

5. What do / does you think of the pet frog?

Exercise 7.4
Circle the sounds to make real words.

1. p___?___ ank / ink

2. pl___?___ ank / ink

3. cr___?___ ank / ink

4. y___?___ ank / ink

5. l___?___ ank / ink

6. r___?___ unk / ash

7. ch___?___ unk / ash

8. spl___?___ unk / ash

9. cr___?___ unk / ash

10. j___?___ unk / ash

Exercise 7.5
Fill in the 'nk' sounds to complete the words below.

1.

t_____ _____ _____

2.

h_____ _____ _____

3.

dr_____ _____ _____

4.

s_____ _____ _____

5.

tr_____ _____ _____

6

b_____ _____ _____

Exercise 8.1
Circle the words that have the /z/ sound (hint, there are 4).

the	his	of	is	this
was	my	he	do	has

Exercise 8.2
Read the sentences to your student saying "blank" for the incomplete words. Then have him/her complete the words using the listed sounds.

These sounds may be used more than once or not at all

ank   enk   ink   onk   unk

1. It is polite to say "please" and "_th_____ you".

2. The truck will _h_____ its horn.

3. The twins slept in _b_____ beds.

4. The mouse ate a _ch_____ of cheese.

5. The girl went to the ice-skating _r_____.

Exercise 8.3
Circle the sounds to make real words.

1. cr__?__ ank / ang

2. bl__?__ unk / ink

3. str__?__ ong / onk

4. str__?__ ink / ing

5. ch__?__ unk / ong

6. cl__?__ ung / ong

Exercise 8.4
Read the sentences to your student saying "blank" for the incomplete words. Then have him/her complete the words using the listed sounds.

These sounds may be used more than once or not at all

ang   eng   ing   ong   ung

1. The bird will __s_____ in the morning.

2. The opposite of short is __l_____.

3. The man sang a __s_____.

4. The lady had a __r_____ on her finger.

5. The bee __st_____ my leg.

6. The bat will __h_____ upside down to sleep.

Exercise 8.5
Complete the words below.

1. w___ ___ ___

2. k___ ___ ___

3. l___ ___ ___

4. t___ ___ ___

5. str___ ___ ___

6. s___ ___ ___

7. tr___ ___ ___

8. dr___ ___ ___

9. r___ ___ ___

10. s___ ___ ___

11. w___ ___ ___

12. sk___ ___ ___

The /ck/ Sounds

Exercise 9.1

Read each sentence to your student, and have him/her complete the sentences with the words that make sense.

stuck   stack   luck

back   trick   brick

1. He played a _____ on me!

2. People think a rabbit's foot is good _____.

3. The sign said that he will be _____ soon.

4. The truck got _____ in the mud.

5. The strong house was made of _____.

6. The boy ate a _____ of pancakes.

Exercise 9.2

Read the words to your student and have him/her circle the correct beginning sounds.

1. __?__ust   tr   chr   5. __?__ip   chr   tr

2. __?__ink   jr   dr   6. __?__op   dr   jr

3. __?__ip   jr   dr   7. __?__ap   chr   tr

4. __?__ag   jr   dr   8. __?__ank   dr   jr

Exercise 9.3
Fill in the 'ck' sounds to complete the words.

1.

s_ _ _ _

6.

tr_ _ _ _

2.

sn_ _ _ _

7.

cl_ _ _ _

3.

s_ _ _ _

8.

bl_ _ _ _

4.

r_ _ _ _

9.

t_ _ _ _

5.

d_ _ _ _

10.

k_ _ _ _

Exercise 9.4
Circle the sounds that make real words.

1. p___?___   ack   etch

2. sw___?___   etch   itch

3. sn___?___   ick   ack

4. sn___?___   uck   ock

5. tr___?___   uck   atch

6. dr___?___   ink   ick

7. tr___?___   ink   ick

8. st___?___   onk   ick

Exercise 9.5
Complete the sentences with the words that make sense.

to   the   have   is

1. The duck _____ in the pond.

2. The truck got stuck in _____ mud.

3. He has _____ go back to the bank.

4. I _____ a lot of luck.

Exercise 10.1
Read the sentences and circle the words that make sense.

1. They will be stung / back at sunset.

2. He must stay / hung and play with his dog.

3. I have to play / check in on my pets.

4. They have to pack / spray for the trip.

5. What is the way / patch   to get back to the camp?

6. She sway / may not want to stop and rest.

Exercise 10.2
Fill in the missing sounds to complete the words.

1. pr__ __

2. t__ __ __

3. tr__ __

4. r__ __ __

5.  cr__ __ __ __

6. s__ __ __

7. l__ __ __

8. w__ __ __

9. d__ __ __

10. tr__ __ __

Exercise 10.3
Circle the sounds to make real words (there is one per line).

1. pr___?___   ath   ank   ack

2. pl___?___   ay   ick   ath

3. shr___?___   ath   ank   ack

4. str___?___   ank   ack   ong

5. st___?___   ong   onk   ick

Exercise 10.4
Read the sentences to your student, saying "blank" for the word in question. Have your student circle the word that makes sense.

1. The dog had no owners, he was a spray / stray.

2. During the storm, the trees sway / play in the wind.

3. The cat likes to pray / play with the string.

4. The bowl was made of bay / clay.

5. They told us to stay / sway until the show was over.

6. The opposite of night is day / may.

7. We will play / pay the waiter for our meal.

Exercise 10.5

Read the clues to your student and have him/her complete the puzzle.

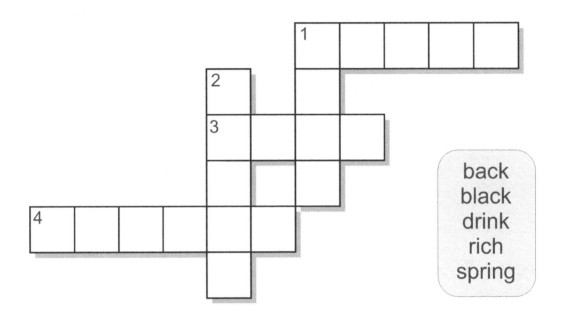

back
black
drink
rich
spring

Across

1. The opposite of white is ___ .
3. The opposite of poor is ___ .
4. The season before summer is ___ .

Down

1. The opposite of front is ___ .
2. Something you do with juice___ .

Exercise R1.1

Write the words for each of the pictures below.

1._____

2._____

3._____

4._____

5._____

Exercise R1.2

Fill in the missing letters for the word below.

1. br__ __ __

4. tr__ __ __

2. cl__ __ __

5. c__ __ __ __

3. t__ __ __

6. br__ __ __

Exercise R1.3
Draw lines to match the words to their pictures.

1. trunk

2. lung

3. sing

4. skunk

5. sink

6. strong

7. drink

8. honk

Exercise R1.4

Read the clues to your student and have him/her write the words, using the clues, on the lines.

1. Change the underlined letter in the word so it becomes something in your body that helps you breathe.

   <u>h</u>ung   _____

2. Change the underlined letters so the word becomes another word for "garbage".

   <u>sm</u>ash _____

3. Change the underlined letters, so the word becomes what your brain does.

   <u>b</u>link   _____

4. Change the underlined letter so the word means opposite of front.

   <u>h</u>ack   _____

5. Change the underlined letters to make the word mean opposite of "go".

   <u>dr</u>op   _____

Exercise R1.5
Read the clues to your student, and have him/her complete the puzzle.

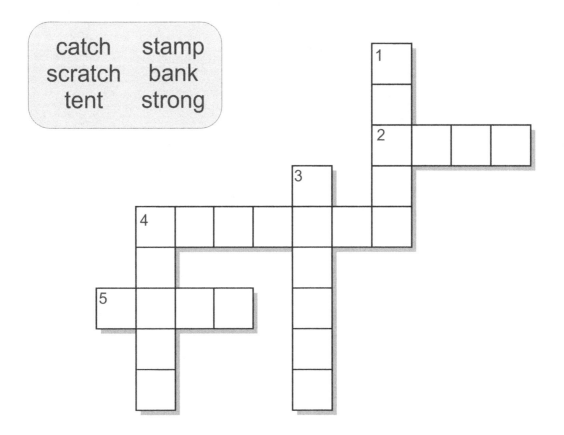

catch   stamp
scratch   bank
tent   strong

Down

1. You use a baseball mitt to __ a ball.

3. The opposite of weak, is __.

4. To send a letter you need a __.

Across

2. When you go camping, you pitch a __.

4. You __ an itch.

5. You put money in a __.

Exercise 11.1
Draw lines to match the rhyming words.

1. bloom	shook
2. group	good
3. flood	gloom
4. took	blood
5. stood	hoop

Exercise 11.2
Complete the sentences with the words that make sense.

food   black   foot
play   hook   frog

1. The witch had a _____ hat.

2. I put the boot on my _____ .

3. The cat will _____ with the string.

4. A _____ may jump into the pool.

5. Put the bags of _____ in the trunk.

6. Hang the hat on the _____ .

Exercise 11.3
Read the following sentences to your student and then have him/her circle the words that make sense.

1. The opposite of "bad" is <u>wood / good</u>.

2. The fish was caught on a <u>hook / book</u>.

3. The past tense of "shake" is <u>shook / shoot</u>.

4. The past tense of "take" is <u>toot / took</u>.

5. Something we do with our eyes is <u>book / look</u>.

Exercise 11.4
Read the following sentences to your student and then have him/her complete the sentences with the words that make sense.

| broom | bedroom | bloom |
| soon | noon | moon |

1. The cow jumped over the _____.

2. People eat lunch at _____ .

3. All my stuff is in my _____ .

4. We sweep the floor with a _____ .

5. In the spring, flowers will _____ .

6. _____ means "at any moment now".

Exercise 11.5
Complete the words below.

1. m__ __ __

2. sp__ __ __

3. br__ __ __

4. f__ __ __

5. h__ __ __

6. b__ __ __

Exercise 11.6
Read each sentence and circle the words that make sense.

1. He swept the room with a boom / broom.

2. She put the book on the plant / shelf.

3. He got mad and took / shook his fist at me.

4. It took a long / good time to get to the bank.

5. She drank the broth with a soon / spoon.

6. Do not look into the sun / moon.

Exercise 12.1
Circle the sounds to make real words (there is one per line).

1. qu_?_	ing	ick	ink
2. st_?_	eck	ay	ush
3. shr_?_	atch	ish	ank
4. th_?_	otch	ish	ink
5. qu_?_	est	an	ing

Exercise 12.2
Read each sentence and complete the missing words with the correct sounds.

ay   oo   ick

1. The dog ran __aw_____.

2. The cat will __pl_____ with the string.

3. The dog will do a __tr_____.

4. I wish I had a __g_____d__ book.

5. He swept the room with a __br_____m__.

6. You must be __qu_____ to catch the rat!

Exercise 12.3

Read the clues to your student and have him/her write the new words on the lines.

1. Change the underlined letters in the word so that it becomes another word for "fast".

   t̲r̲ick _____

2. Change underlined letters in the word so it becomes something a duck says.

   t̲r̲ack _____

3. Change the word so that it becomes the name of the utensil that you use to eat ice-cream and soup.

   moon _____

4. Change the word so it becomes something that you use to sweep with.

   room _____

5. Change the underlined letter in the word so it becomes something you eat.

   m̲ood _____

6. Change the underlined letters in the word so it becomes the word for when you want to stop doing something.

   quiz̲ _____

Exercise 12.4
Read the sentences and circle the matching pictures.

1. They say this brings good luck.

2. He is looking at his book.

3. He sat at a desk and took a quiz.

4. The cat was quick to catch the rat.

5. He hung his hat on the hook.

6. Put the quilt on the bed.

Exercise 13.1
Complete the words below with the 'nch' sounds.

1. 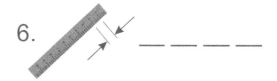 wr__ __ __ __

2. p__ __ __ __

3. b__ __ __ __

4. br__ __ __ __

5. l__ __ __ __

6. __ __ __ __

Exercise 13.2
Read the sentences to your student and have him/her complete the words with the sounds listed.

> ick   ank   oo   uck   anch   inch   ack

1. We saw a chimp at the z_____.

2. My grandmother likes to p_____ my cheeks.

3. The birds were perched on a br_____.

4. If you eat too much, you may get s_____.

5. There was a cr_____ in the sidewalk.

6. Our car got st_____ in the snow.

7. Fill in the bl_____ to answer the question.

Exercise 13.3
Read the sentences and complete the words.

uck   ong   atch   etch   ank   ack

1. The chick will soon h__ __ __ __ .

2. On the trip, I want to sit in the b__ __ __ of the van.

3. Wish me good l__ __ __ on my test.

4. My dog will play f__ __ __ __ with me.

5. My pants shr__ __ __ in the wash.

6. The str__ __ __ man will lift the box.

Exercise 13.4
Circle the sounds to make real words (there is one per line).

1. p_?_	unch	anch	ench
2. p_?_	onch	ench	inch
3. br_?_	inch	anch	onch
4. st_?_	otch	itch	atch
5. bl_?_	ick	uck	ack
6. sw_?_	oo	ay	ick

Exercise 13.5

Read the following clues to your student, and have him/her write the new words on the lines provided.

1. Change the underlined letter to finish the sentence: A magician does a magic ___.

tr<u>u</u>ck _____

2. Change the underlined letter in the word to make it something you sit on in a park.

b<u>u</u>nch _____

3. Change the underlined letter in the word to make it something that you find in a library.

<u>t</u>ook _____

4. Change the underlined letter in the word to make it something someone does when they tightly squeeze your skin with their fngers.

p<u>u</u>nch _____

5. Change the underlined letter in the word so it becomes the opposite of bad.

<u>h</u>ood _____

Exercise 14.1

Read each sentence to your student, using the word "blank" for the missing words. Have him/her complete the sentences with the words below.

fly	why	cry	night
shy	try	by	right

1. He will _____ to jump over the puddle.

2. We go to bed at _____.

3. The baby will _____ when he's hungry.

4. The little boy was very _____ around new people.

5. The opposite of left is _____.

6. The story was written _____ a little girl.

7. _____ did the girl have to leave early?

8. This summer, we will _____ on an airplane.

Exercise 14.2

Circle a sound to make a real word.

1. th_?_ onk ink	4. sh_?_ igh y
2. th_?_ igh ath	5. sh_?_ ack ath
3. th_?_ ack ing	6. sh_?_ unk ock

Exercise 14.3
Read the clues to your student and have him/her circle the answer.

1. The opposite of low is: high / shy

2. The opposite of day is: sky / night

4. The opposite of wet is: dry / fry

5. The opposite of dim is: sight / bright

6. The opposite of wrong is: fight / right

Exercise 14.4
Read the sentences and choose the correct sounds to complete the missing words.

uck   ock   ick   unk   ank

1. The fish swam in the __t_____ .

2. My foot got __st_____ in the mud.

3. The twins had __b_____ beds.

4. I put my foot in the __s_____ .

5. The dog will fetch the __st_____ .

Exercise 14.5
Draw lines to match the words to their pictures.

1. thigh

2. sunlight

3. fight

4. spy

5. night

6. cry

7. fly

8. fry

Exercise 15.1

Read the sentences and complete the missing words using a sound listed. Note that the sounds in the box may be used more than once or not at all.

ank igh inch ench oy oi oo

1. Bring the soup to a b___ ___ l.

2. I sat on the b___ ___ ___ ___ to rest.

3. Wrap the sandwich in tinf___ ___l.

4. The b___ ___s will play in the back of the room.

5. Put the plant into the s___ ___l.

6. We dr___ ___ ___ milk with the snack.

7. A wrench is a t___ ___l.

8. He kept his t___ ___s in the red box.

Exercise 15.2
Complete the words below.

1.   c _ _ _

5.   p_ _ _ _

2.   sw_ _ _ _

6.   p_ _ _ _

3.   t_ _ box

7.   dr_ _ _

4.   b_ _

8.   c_ _ _

Exercise 15.3
Circle the words that make the most sense.

1. He will try to catch a fish / lamp with his net.

2. He wants to scoop the sand into the bucket / pool .

3. He will join / broil the fish for lunch.

4. She put the quilt on the bed / skunk.

5. She will toss the coin / kitten into the well.

6. He wants to shoot chimps / hoops today.

7. We went for a swim in the drool / pool .

Exercise 15.4

Read the following clues to your student, and have him/her write the new words on the lines provided.

1. Change the underlined letter so the word becomes the opposite of "loose".

<u>n</u>ight   _____

2. Change the underlined letter in the word to make it something that water does when it gets very hot.

<u>c</u>oil   _____

3. Change the underlined letter in the word to make it another word that means "happy".

<u>b</u>oy   _____

4. Change the underlined letter so the word becomes one that describes a hammer or screw driver.

<u>f</u>ool   _____

5. Change the underlined letter in the word so it becomes the singular word for "teeth".

<u>b</u>ooth   _____

Exercise 16.1
Complete the words below (each word has the /ar/ sound).

1. st __ __

2. c __ __

3. b __ __ __

4. j __ __

5. sh __ __ __

6. ch __ __ __

7. c __ __ __ s

8. __ __ __

Exercise 16.2
Complete the words below (each word has the /or/ sound).

Remember, many words that end with the /or/ sound have a "do nothing" 'e' at the end.

1. c __ __ __

2. st __ __ __

3. c __ __ __

4. th __ __ __

5. sn __ __ __

6. h __ __ __ e

7. h __ __ __

8. sc __ __ __

Exercise 16.3
Draw lines to match the words with their pictures.

1. th<u>ir</u>d

2. ch<u>ur</u>ch

3. sk<u>ir</u>t

4. f<u>ir</u>st

5. sh<u>ir</u>t

6. s<u>ur</u>f

7. b<u>ir</u>d

8. t<u>ur</u>n

Exercise 16.4
Read the sentences and circle the words that make sense.

1. Her car is not far from the <u>snore / store</u>.

2. He has a black <u>marker / core</u> in his box.

3. They have no <u>more / dark</u> snacks on the shelf.

4. She wore a pink skirt to <u>church / porch</u>.

5. The smart boy will <u>curl / turn</u> the light on.

6. He got a sunburn at the <u>market / shore</u>.

7. Turn the car so you do not hit the <u>curb / charm</u>.

Exercise 16.5
The words below have **extra letters** that are not needed.
Each word has the /or/ sound. Cross out the unused letters.

door   floor   poor   your   four

Exercise 16.6
Read the sentences and circle the words that make sense.

1. The stars <u>was / were</u> in the night sky.

2. The night <u>was / were</u> cool.

3. <u>Were / We're</u> going to the park.

4. The girl <u>was / were</u> in her bedroom.

5. The group of kids <u>was / were</u> in the pool.

Exercise 17.1
Draw lines to match the pictures to the words.

1. p<u>ow</u>er

2. <u>ow</u>l

3. cl<u>ow</u>n

4. cl<u>ou</u>d

5. sh<u>ou</u>t

6. m<u>ou</u>se

Exercise 17.2
Circle the picture that goes with the word.

1.	bow			
2.	bowl			
3.	blow			
4.	crow			
5.	flower			
6.	shower			
7.	house			
8.	mouth			
9.	cow			

Exercise 17.3
Read the sentences and choose the correct sounds to complete the missing words.

ay   oo   or   ar   ur   ou   ow

1. His house is not too far from t__ __ n .

2. After the st__ __m, we lost our power.

3. Do you think an owl is sm__ __t ?

4. What was the girl shouting ab__ __t ?

5. Park the car next to the c__ __ b .

6. At lunch, they put the food on a tr__ __ .

7. The loose t__ __ th is in my mouth.

Exercise 17.4
Circle the sounds that make real words.

1. p__?__l   oo   ou   4. r__?__   ar   ow

2. cl__?__d   oo   ou   5. bl__?__   ar   ow

3. st__?__t   oo   ou   6. f__?__   ar   ow

Exercise 17.5
Circle the words that make sense for each sentence below.

1. The boy will throw the bat on the <u>cloud / ground</u>.

2. How long did the girl sit on the <u>stool / clown</u> ?

3. The drums <u>were / was</u> loud.

4. The girl got lost in the <u>crown / crowd</u> .

5. If you follow the boy you might get <u>lost / snow</u>.

6. My father does not <u>mow / own</u> a red car.

7. In the winter, it might <u>snow / shout</u>.

8. We're about to have our <u>crow / lunch</u>.

9. We found a red dog <u>horse / house</u> for our dog.

10. The boy took a <u>shower / shouting</u> in the morning.

Exercise 18.1

For each line, circle the sound that makes a real word.

1. b_?_	orn	ew
2. t_?_	oin	own
3. gr_?_	ore	ew
4. fl_?_	ew	ay
5. scr_?_	ow	ew

Exercise 18.2

Read the sentences to your student and have him/her write the correct words on the lines provided. Not all words in the box below are used.

drew	threw	shower	could
row	bowl	crew	flew

1. I wish I _____ go to the zoo.

2. The baseball player _____ the ball.

3. The birds _____ away.

4. Instead of a bath, I will take a _____.

5. The ship had a _____ of ten sailors.

6. On a cold day, it's nice to have a _____ of soup.

7. The boy _____ pictures with crayons.

Exercise 18.3
Circle the word that is correctly spelled and read it out loud.

1. tirn / turn	4. boyl / boil
2. croud / crowd	5. houl / howl
3. bloo / blew	6. grew / groo

Exercise 18.4
Circle the *three* words that have the **long 'i'** sound.

play	try	right	high
bang	fool	tray	boil

Exercise 18.5
Circle the sounds that match (there is one per line).

1.	er	oo	oy	ir	ow
2.	ew	oo	oy	ir	ow
3.	ou	oo	oy	ir	ow
4.	ur	oo	oy	ir	ow
5.	oi	oo	oy	ir	ow

Exercise 18.6
Circle the *four* words that rhyme with "wood".

food	stood	pool
could	should	tool
droop	cool	hood

Exercise 19.1
Read the sentences and circle the words that make sense.

1. Tack / Take a look at his new car.

2. Pound the stack / stake into the ground.

3. They want to swim in the lack / lake.

4. He will rake / rack up points in his game.

5. The girl will try to back / bake a cake.

6. After lunch we will have a snake / snack.

Exercise 19.2
Use the **V**CV rule to find the long vowels in the letter groups below. Draw arrows from the second vowel to the first vowel that gets turned long. Underline the long vowel.

1. pota

3. amibr

5. umotx

7. lobut

2. stimog

4. opit

6. imat

8. flita

Exercise 19.3

First read the words in the box below, and then complete the sentences with the words that make sense. Not all words are used.

rip	shin	rod	fin	tub	kit
ripe	shine	rode	fine	tube	kite

1. Another word for "good" is _____.

2. When I take a bath, I go into my _____.

3. She _____ a brown horse.

4. At the park, we flew a _____.

5. If your pants are too tight, they may _____.

6. In the morning, the sun will _____.

7. I will make a bird house with a _____.

8. She put the blood into a test- _____.

9. A kick in the _____ can hurt.

10. The man had shark _____ soup.

Exercise 19.4
Fill in the vowel pairs for the **common** long vowel teams.

Exercise 19.5
Complete the words with a **common** long vowel team.

1. We might take the b___ ___t on the lake tonight.

2. The girl broke her fingern___ ___l.

3. We will make pumpkin p___ ___.

4. If something is not false then it is tr___ ___.

5. It might r___ ___n later today.

6. The dog always wags his t___ ___l.

7. I like to fl___ ___t on the tube in the pool.

8. I had a p___ ___n in my neck from watching the game.

9. The ink from the pen may st___ ___n your shirt.

10. Our flag is red, white and bl___ ___.

Exercise 19.6
Circle the words that make sense in the sentences below.

1. My teacher said to be quite / quiet.

2. My dad wore a blue suit / fruit to work.

3. The lion / line will roar at the crowd.

4. The ink from the pen will ruin / paint your shirt.

5. The poet will read her diet / poem to us.

6. Put the fruit / suit in the basket.

Exercise 19.7
Complete the words with the sounds below.

> ar   ir   oi   ou   ai   ee

1. The king and qu___ ___n sat on a throne.

2. The dog ran around the y___ ___d.

3. The b___ ___d sat up high on a branch.

4. He broke his finger right on the j___ ___nt.

5. The pig stuck his sn___ ___t into the food bucket.

6. The house needs a new coat of p___ ___nt .

Exercise 19.8
Circle the sounds that make real words.

1. fl_?___	ow	ou	ew
2. gr_?___	own	oi	ew
3. ch_?___	ore	ew	ir

Exercise 20.1
Fill in the vowel pairs for the common long vowel teams.

a	e	i	o	u
☐	☐	☐	☐	☐
	☐			

Exercise 20.2
Choose the words that make sense, and then add the ending 'ing' to the words to complete the sentences.

1. The boy was _____ the nail with a hammer.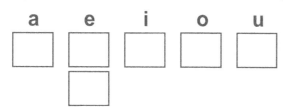
   pet   hit

2. The girl was _____ into a hamburger.
   bite   dive

3. I was _____ to see you later.
   hope   like

4. The rabbit was _____ away from us.
   sit   hop

5. The woman was _____ a drink.
   sip   mop

Exercise 20.3
Complete the words below.

1. tr__ __

2. p__ __

3. sn__ k__

4. t__p__

5. t__ __l

6. tr__ __n

7. p__ __l

8. t__ __

Exercise 20.4
Add 'ing' to the words below.

ing

1. take _____

2. part _____

3. cry _____

4. sit _____

5. pet _____

6. like _____

7. melt _____

8. sing _____

Exercise 20.5
Circle the letters that make the sound indicated on the left. There may be one or two answers.

1. What makes a long 'a' ?	ay	igh	ai
2. What makes a long 'e' ?	ee	oy	ea
3. What makes a long 'i' ?	igh	ie	oi
4. What makes a long 'o' ?	oo	oa	oy
5. What makes a long 'u' ?	ue	oy	ou

Exercise R2.1
Read and complete the sentences below.

1. The boy grew an i __ __ __ last year.

2. Carrots, peas and beef are used to make st__ __.

3. The playset had a swing and a sl__ __ __.

4. Trees are planted in the gr__ __ __ __.

5. Cars and trucks can drive on the r__ __ __.

Exercise R2.2
Circle the words that are correctly spelled and read them out loud.

1. shirt / shurt

2. stor / store

3. therd / third

4. were / wer

5. turn / tirn

6. ferst / first

Exercise R2.3
Write the words for each picture below.

VCV Words

1. _____

2. _____

3. _____

4. _____

5. _____

6. _____

VV Words

7. _____

8. _____

9. _____

10. _____

11. _____

12. _____

Exercise R2.4

Read the sentences and circle the words that have the correct vowel teams for the long 'e' sound.

1. I <u>feel / feal</u> sick today.

2. If it is not fake, then it is <u>reel / real</u>.

3. There are seven days in a <u>week / weak</u>.

4. At night we go to <u>sleep / sleap</u>.

5. My house is just down the <u>street / streat</u>.

Exercise R2.5

Compete the sentences below.

1. The horse is in the b___ ___n.

2. The farmer grew a lot of c___ ___n.

3. At night we wish on a st___ ___.

4. There is nothing inside the j___ ___.

5. The red b___ ___ was in my hair.

6. The sp___ ___n is next to the bowl.

7. You must sweep the floor with the br___ ___m.

8. The king always wore a cr___ ___n.

Exercise R2.6

Complete each sentence by adding the word for what the pictures are doing. For all words you will have to add 'ing'.

ing

1. The boy is _____.

2. The hands are _____.

3. The baby is _____.

4. The deer is _____.

5. The dog is _____.

6. The man is _____.

Exercise 21.1
Circle the ending sound for each word.

1. clapped /t/ or /ed/	6. wished /t/ or /ed/
2. twisted /t/ or /ed/	7. flashed /t/ or /ed/
3. shopped /t/ or /ed/	8. kicked /t/ or /ed/
4. flopped /t/ or /ed/	9. rested /t/ or /ed/
5. clicked /t/ or /ed/	10. handed /t/ or /ed/

Exercise 21.2
Write the words below in their **past tense** form.

ed

1. skip _____

2. shop _____

3. plan _____

4. rip _____

5. drag _____

Don't forget us!

Exercise 21.3

Read the sentences and write the words in the correct tense (past or present) on the lines.

1. The boy is __ __ __ __ __ __. cry

2. The sad girl __ __ __ __ __ last night. cry

3. He __ __ __ __ __ to open the jar. try

4. She was __ __ __ __ __ __ to read to the boy. try

5. They ate __ __ __ __ __ chicken for dinner. fry

6. The fish was __ __ __ __ __ __ in the pan. fry

Exercise 21.4

Draw lines to match each word to its **past tense** form.

1.	eat	took
2.	make	flew
3.	shake	dug
4.	fly	ate
5.	draw	kept
6.	take	drew
7.	keep	shook
8.	dig	made

Exercise 21.5

Circle the words that make sense, and then write the past tense form of the words on the lines.

1. He _____ at the bug with a stick.

   sit   poke

2. The children _____ in the snow.

   eat   play

3. We _____ for the bus to pick us up.

   wait   dream

4. We _____ the fish swim in the tank.

   watch   drop

5. Yesterday, my mother _____ a cake.

   bake   lick

6. I went to get my hair _____ .

   pick   trim

Exercise 22.1
Fill in the blanks to complete the words in the sentences below.

> and   end   ind   ond   und

1. I would rather sit than st__ __ __.

2. Ducks and fish swim in the p__ __ __.

3. I need to f__ __ __ my suitcase for the trip.

4. Look __ __ __er the bed for your socks.

5. I sp__ __ __ a lot of time at school.

Exercise 22.2
Circle the words that make sense for the sentences below.

1. We're / Were going to send the letter today.

2. She said we're / were leaving at the end of June.

3. We where / were staying over his house for dinner.

4. Were / Where the children hiding under the blankets?

5. Were / Where are the birds finding food in the winter?

Exercise 22.3
Circle the answer to the questions below.

What letters make...

1. the long 'o' sound?   oi   oa

2. the long 'o' sound?   ow   oi

3. the /ou/ sound as in "ouch"?   oi   ow

4. the long 'a' sound?   ie   ai

5. the long 'a' sound?   ay   oa

6. the long 'i' sound?   igh   oi

Exercise 22.4
Complete the sentences so that they make sense.

1. She _____ the nametag onto his shirt.
   pin

2. The girl was _____ down the street.
   run

3. The boy _____ into the pool.
   jump

4. The pilot _____ the plane on the runway.
   land

5. The girls were _____ the game.
   win

Exercise 22.5
Circle the words that have the long 'i' sound (there are 6).

fly   child   list   winning   find

sight   shin   wild   cry   mint

Exercise 22.6
Circle the words that are correctly spelled.

1. rane / rain   6. return / retern

2. shirt / shurt   7. clowd / cloud

3. jumpt / jumped   8. town / toun

4. hurt / hirt   9. were / wer

5. shopt / shopped   10. street / streat

Exercise 22.7
In the letter groups below, underline the vowels that are long due to the **V**V or **V**C**V** long vowel rules (there are 3).

gidde   smitbe   bito

higip   guebt   anpe

The /ct/ Sounds

Exercise 23.1
Complete the sentences with the sounds below. Sounds may be used more than once or not at all.

> act   ect   ict   oct   uct

1. Conn___ ___ ___ the dots.

2. The man will be ___ ___ ___ing in the play.

3. You can sel___ ___ ___ where we go for dinner.

4. She says that she can pred___ ___ ___ what will happen.

5. The woman is a susp___ ___ ___ in the crime.

6. The loud man was ej___ ___ ___ed from the game.

Exercise 23.2
Circle the words that make sense. Be careful; sometimes a past tense word sounds like a 'ct' word.

1. The dog lict / licked my hand.

2. The car bact / backed down the driveway.

3. The boys made a pact / packed to always be friends.

4. She dropped the cup on the floor and it cract / cracked.

Exercise 23.3
Complete the sentences below so that they make sense.

1. The boy _____ on the banana peel.
   slip

2. The girl _____ to look over the railing.
   try

3. The child _____ an object on the beach.
   find

4. The boy _____ mean to us.
   act

5. The dog was _____ away from the girl.
   run

6. The dirty boy _____ a bubble bath in the tub.
   take

7. The children _____ on the teachers.
   spy

8. The child _____ down the road.
   skip

9. We _____ up our things for the trip.
   pack

10. The bird _____ away from us.
    fly

Exercise 23.4
Read the sentences and circle the matching pictures.

1. The teacher good, but she is strict.

2. He is the conductor

3. The farmer rides on a tractor.

4. The man will collect our trash.

5. The inspector looked for clues.

6. The doctor helped the sick man.

7. An insect landed on my hand.

Exercise 24.1

Draw lines to match the words to their pictures.

1. crawl

2. saw

3. paw

4. draw

5. haunt

6. claw

7. straw

8. yawn

Exercise 24.2
Draw lines to match the words to their pictures.

1. ball

2. wall

3. fall

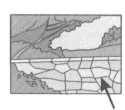

4. walk

5. talk

6. chalk

Exercise 24.3
Complete the sentences with the words that make sense.

walk   ball   awful   pause   fault

1. It was my _____ we were late for the show.

2. She likes to _____ her dog down the street.

3. The dog chased the _____ that I threw.

4. Burnt toast smells _____.

5. You can stop the song by pressing _____.

Exercise 24.4
Draw lines to match the sounds.

1. igh   ai

2. aw   oi

3. oy   oo

4. ew   er

5. ay   ie

6. ur   au

Exercise 24.5
Complete the sentences with the words that make sense.

because	lawn	launch	dawn
subject	predict	author	drawn

1. The _____ wrote a book about animals.

2. I like baseball _____ it is fun!

3. My best _____ is math.

4. The opposite of dusk is _____ .

5. I tried to _____ what will happen next.

6. My father has to mow the _____ .

7. We went to the _____ to watch the rocket blast off.

Exercise 25.1
Draw lines to match the words to their pictures.

1. toes

2. nose

3. pose

4. rose

5. hose

Exercise 25.2
Fill in the missing letters to complete the words below.

1. h__ __ __ __

2. h__ __ __ __

3.  n__ __ __ __

4. m__ __ __ __

Exercise 25.3
Circle the words that make sense in the sentences below.

1. The _mouse / blouse_ took the cheese from the trap.

2. It is polite to say _pause / please_ and thank you.

3. It is fun to ride on a _house / horse_.

4. My _house / horse_ is just around the block.

5. My loud brother made a lot of _nose / noise_.

6. She _chose / choose_ to go home at nine o'clock.

7. They will use the lid to _clues / close_ the jar.

Exercise 25.4
Complete the sentences below so that they make sense.

1. The boy is _____ soap to wash his hands.
   <u>use</u>

2. The girl _____ when her dog was lost.
   <u>cry</u>

3. We _____ the map to get around town.
   <u>use</u>

4. They _____ our car at the border.
   <u>stop</u>

5. I am _____ and locking the door.
   <u>close</u>

Exercise 25.5
Circle the **seven** words below where the 's' has the /z/ sound.

the<u>se</u>	u<u>se</u>	cha<u>se</u>
tho<u>se</u>	hi<u>s</u>	wi<u>se</u>
ca<u>se</u>	nur<u>se</u>	crea<u>se</u>
hou<u>se</u>	pur<u>se</u>	pau<u>se</u>
hor<u>se</u>	becau<u>se</u>	loo<u>se</u>

Exercise 25.6
Complete the sentences below so that they make sense.

1. The mouse _____ its way out of the box.

claw

2. The snake _____ up and hissed at us.

coil

3. I had a hard time _____ a good song to sing.

choose

4. The boy was _____ like he knew what to do.

act

5. The child _____ behind the bush.

crawl

Exercise 25.7
Circle the matching sounds; there is one per line.

1. aw	oa	ai	au
2. oi	oy	ou	aw
3. oo	oa	ew	ow
4. ou	ow	oi	ue
5. ie	ai	ew	igh

Exercise 26.1
Circle the words that make sense in the sentences.

1. What <u>type / crazy</u> of pie is your favorite?

2. The brown blanket is ugly but it is <u>funny / cozy</u>.

3. I went to the <u>bakery / pantry</u> to buy donuts.

4. We had to <u>supply / deny</u> the camp with food and water.

5. Try not to be <u>noisy / silly</u> when people are sleeping.

6. The <u>creepy / sneaky</u> dog stole meat from the young boy.

7. It is a <u>mystery / symbol</u> where the candy went.

Exercise 26.2
Draw lines to match the words to their pictures.

1. lady

2. pony

3. monkey

4. money

5. baby

6. itchy

7. key

8. fly

9. spy

10. cry

Exercise 26.3
Circle the words that make sense in the sentences below.

1. The haunted house was <u>crunchy / scary</u>.

2. I cannot <u>deny / supply</u> that I ate the peach pie.

3. I have to <u>comply / rely</u> on my lungs to breathe.

4. We waited for the paint to <u>modify / dry</u>.

5. The meal did not <u>satisfy / supply</u> my hunger.

6. He tried to <u>pry / dry</u> the lid off the jar.

7. We got <u>party / plenty</u> of rain last September.

8. We have to <u>worry / hurry</u> to catch the airplane.

9. We had to <u>modify / classify</u> our plans for dinner.

10. The <u>crazy / lazy</u> monkey ran off with my yellow hat.

Adding 'ly' and 'er'

Exercise 27.1
Add the ending 'ly' to the words below.

ly

1. _____
   normal

2. _____
   final

3. _____
   safe

4. _____
   lucky

5. _____
   angry

6. _____
   happy

Exercise 27.2
Circle the words that make sense in the sentences below.

1. We quietly tip-toed through the library / kangaroo.

2. The baby quickly grabbed his mailbox / bottle.

3. The cook slowly stirred the soup / donkey.

4. The singer softly sang a bagel / song.

5. He really likes to eat turkey sandwiches / baskets.

Exercise 27.3
Add the ending 'er' to the words below.

er

1. hot   _____

2. big   _____

3. fat   _____

4. hit   _____

5. jog   _____

Exercise 27.4
Add the ending 'er' to the words below.

er

1. happy _____

2. funny _____

3. ugly _____

4. sorry _____

5. pretty _____

When 'g' has the /j/ Sound

Exercise 28.1

Circle the sound that the 'ge', 'gi' or 'gy' makes in the words below. If you don't know, try the 'g' as a /g/ and a /j/.

1. <u>g</u>em   /j/ or /g/   3. hun<u>ge</u>r   /j/ or /g/

2. <u>g</u>irl   /j/ or /g/   4. dan<u>ge</u>r   /j/ or /g/

Exercise 28.2

Circle the sounds that make real words.

1. j<u> ? </u>	udge	adge		5. pl<u> ? </u>	edge	idge
2. br<u> ? </u>	edge	idge		6. b<u> ? </u>	adge	edge
3. l<u> ? </u>	edge	adge		7. w<u> ? </u>	adge	edge
4. sl<u> ? </u>	adge	udge		8. gr<u> ? </u>	udge	adge

Exercise 28.3
Fill in the blanks with the words that make sense in the sentences.

> wedge   judge   stage   edge   huge

1. The actor walked up on the _____.

2. Another word for "big" is _____ .

3. The diver stood on the _____ of the cliff.

4. I'll have a _____ of cheddar cheese.

5. In a court-room, you will find a _____.

Exercise 28.4
Circle the word that makes sense for each sentence.

1. Emily is <u>plunging / changing</u> into her bathing suit.

2. Her job is to <u>arrange / plunge</u> the flowers in the vase.

3. The angry man said he would get <u>napkins/ revenge</u>.

4. They said that we should not talk to <u>strangers / dangers</u>.

5. The lines come together to make an <u>angel / angle</u>.

6. When the ball came at me, I <u>cringed / plunged</u>.

Exercise 28.5
Circle the sounds that make real words.

1. cr__?__   ange   inge

2. arr__?__   ange   inge

3. str__?__   ange   inge

4. tw__?__   ange   inge

5. pl__?__   unge   inge

6. l__?__   unge   inge

7. b__?__   unge   inge

8. fr__?__   unge   inge

Exercise 28.6
Complete the words below.

1. f__ __ __ __

2. pl __ __ __ er

3. an__ __ __

4. fr__ __ __ __

5. br__ __ __ __

6. b __ __ __ __

Exercise 29.1
Circle the words that make sense in the sentences below.

1. What <u>percent / advice</u> of three hundred is fifty-five?

2. What <u>circle / advice</u> did the lady give you?

3. What is the <u>dance / chance</u> of rain for today?

4. Where is the best <u>place / space</u> to hang my coat?

5. Why was the <u>choice / price</u> of the fruit so high?

Exercise 29.2
Circle the sounds that make a real word. There may be more than one correct answer for each line.

1. pl___?___   ace   ice

2. f___?___   ace   ice

3. r___?___   ace   ice

4. sp___?___   ace   ice

5. gr___?___   ace   ice

6. sl___?___   ace   ice

7. adv___?___   ace   ice

8. p___?___   ace   ice

Exercise 29.3

Circle the sounds that make a real word. There may be more than one correct answer for each line.

1. gl__?__   ance   ange

2. ch__?__   ance   ange

3. pr__?__   ance   ange

4. r__?__   ance   ange

5. tr__?__   ance   ange

Exercise 29.4

Complete the words in the sentences below using the sounds in the box.

> ice   ace   ance   ence   ince

1. The boy ran in the _r_____.

2. I ordered a _sl_____ of peach pie.

3. My mouth and nose are part of my _f_____.

4. I have not seen him _s_____ last year.

5. The rocket blasted off into _sp_____.

6. We enjoyed watching the lady _d_____.

7. The new teacher was very _n_____ to me.

8. The _f_____ keeps our dog in the yard.

9. Asking others for _adv_____ makes sense.

10. _Pl_____ your belongings into the bag.

Exercise 29.5
Complete the sentences below so that they make sense.

1. The lady was _____ on the stage.
   dance

2. The girl _____ a gift in the mail.
   receive

3. The deer _____ around the woods.
   prance

4. The player was _____ to the next level.
   advance

5. The child _____ the image on the paper.
   trace

Exercise 29.6
Circle the four words below where 'g' sounds like /j/.

raged	forged	energy	get
bagged	foggy	clingy	gerbil

Exercise 30.1

Read the words to your student and have him/her use the /k/ rule to determine the correct way to spell each word.

1.	skill	scill	5.	piknik	picnic
2.	kind	cind	6.	keep	ceep
3.	klap	clap	7.	klear	clear
4.	traffik	traffic	8.	kamp	camp

Exercise 30.2

Fill in the boxes with the sound that each 'c' makes and then read the word out loud.

'k' or 's'

1. □□ accent
2. □ bounce
3. □ mercy
4. □□ accident
5. □□ success
6. □□ accept

Exercise 30.3
Complete the sentences with the words that make sense.

fantastic   plastic   traffic   attic

romantic   garlic   magic   panic

1. We found the kitten hiding up in the _____.

2. The cook chopped the _____.

3. Do not _____ if you are in an accident.

4. Terrific and _____ mean the same thing.

5. The _____ toy easily broke.

6. My parents went out for a _____ dinner.

7. There was a lot of _____ on the highway.

8. We saw a _____ show at school today.

Exercise R3.1
Match the sounds on the left with the sounds on the right.

1.	ce		/aw/
2.	au		/awl/
3.	adge		/aj/
4.	alk		/s/
5.	all		/awk/

Exercise R3.2
Complete the crossword puzzle.

pause
fault
claws
predict
false

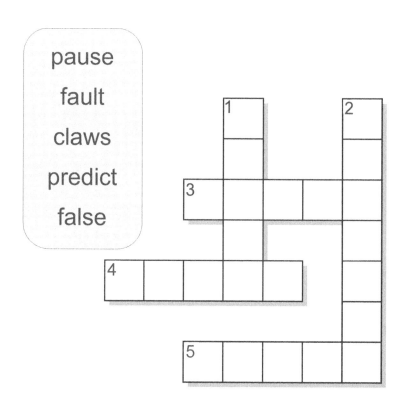

Down

1. A cat has sharp __.
2. A fortune teller
   may __ the future.

Across

3. You can play, __ or
   stop a video.
4. If it is not true,
   then it is __ .
5. Do not blame me,
   it is not my __ .

Exercise R3.3
Complete the sentences with the words that make sense.

law	talk	doctor
chalk	symbol	traffic

1. When you get sick, you see a _____.

2. The teacher wrote on the board with _____.

3 To stay out of jail, you follow the _____.

4. The car accident caused a lot of _____.

5. Another word for "chat" is _____.

6. The flag is a _____ of our country.

Exercise R3.4
Answer the questions below.

1. 'g' *sometimes* is /j/ when followed by: ___ ___ ___

2. 'c' *always* is /s/ when followed by: ___ ___ ___

3. When 'y' is in the **middle** of a word, it can sound like:

long ___ or short ___

4. When 'y' is at the **end** of a word it can sound like:

long ___ or long ___

Exercise R3.5
Fill in the blanks to spell the words for the pictures below.

1. j _ _ _ _

5. b _ _ n _ _

2. c _ _ _

6.  pen _ _ _

3. b _ _ _ _

7. jui_ _ _

4. br _ _ _ _

8. pr_ _ _

Exercise R3.6
Add 'ly' to the words and write the new word on the line.

ly

1. soft _____

4. easy _____

2. swift _____

5. final _____

3. late _____

6. lucky _____

Exercise R3.7
Complete the sentences with the words that make sense.

choice	space	principal	chance
force	city	fence	race

1. The drawer does not have a lot of _____ for all of my socks.

2. There is a sixty percent _____ of rain for today.

3. Do not _____ me to go out when I am sick.

4. Every year we go to the _____ to see a show.

5. The large dog jumped over the _____ .

6. Our teacher gave us a _____ on what to do for homework.

7. The _____ of our school is very strict.

8. The _____ car zoomed around the track.

Exercise 31.1

First read the words in the box below. Then complete the sentences with the **plural form** of the words that make sense.

> house - houses   lady - ladies
> box - boxes   cherry - cherries
> lash - lashes   try - tries
> wolf - wolves   puppy - puppies

1. The boy stacked the _____ on the shelf.

2. The girl had long eye- _____ .

3. The _____ roamed the hills in packs.

4. There were a lot of _____ in the litter.

5. How many _____ are on your block?

6. We picked a bunch of _____ from the tree.

7. All of the _____ came over for lunch.

8. They gave us three _____ to pass the test.

Exercise 31.2

For each sentence, choose the word that make sense and then make the word plural.

1. How many _____ to you need for packing?

        box   frog

2. There are seven _____ in a week.

        insect   day

3. In the fall, we had to rake the _____ .

        leaf   nest

4. We were granted three _____ .

        wish   dish

5. The boy likes bedtime _____ .

        price   story

Exercise 31.3

Read the hints below, and then circle the words that the hints describe.

1. When you do not know something, it is a __.

    story   fact   mystery

2. If you do not know someone, they are a __.

    stranger   person   stringer

3. Some people may offer you __.

    advise   advance   advice

4. Birds often eat __.

    burry   berries   berry

Exercise 31.4
Write the words below in their plural form.

1. tax _____

2. bush _____

3. lash _____

4. memory _____

5. story _____

Exercise 31.5
Circle the sounds that the underlined letters make.

1. cakes	/k/	/s/		5. changes	/g/	/j/
2. cities	/k/	/s/		6. begins	/g/	/j/
3. chances	/k/	/s/		7. oranges	/g/	/j/
4. picnics	/k/	/s/		8. charges	/g/	/j/

Exercise 32.1
Write the number of syllables you hear in the words below.

1. funny ☐   5. arrange ☐

2. yellow ☐   6. hunger ☐

3. smudge ☐   7. energy ☐

4. mystery ☐   8. angrier ☐

Exercise 32.2
Write the words for the pictures below. Note that all of the words are FLOSS words.

1. _ _ _ _ _

2. _ _ _ _ _

3. _ _ _ _ _

4. _ _ _ _

5. _ _ _ _

6. _ _ _ _

7. _ _ _ _

8. _ _ _ _

Exercise 32.3
Circle the word that makes sense for each sentence.

1. The broken toy was <u>endless / useless</u>.

2. I sleep on a <u>mattress / fortress</u>.

3. The judge called the <u>waitress / witness</u> up to his bench.

4. After lunch, we went outside for <u>success / recess</u>.

5. Do not be <u>careless / skinless</u> when doing your work.

6. When I clean my room, it is <u>distress / spotless</u>.

Exercise 32.4
Change the words to their **past tense** forms.

Today I _____, but yesterday I _____.

1. tell _____

2. hold _____

3. post _____

4. fold _____

5. sell _____

6. roll _____

Exercise 32.5
Circle the word that makes sense for each sentence below.

1. The basket holds all of the <u>berries / houses</u>.

2. When it is cold, the store sells many <u>ghosts / scarves</u>.

3. The bus held most of the <u>children / hamburgers</u>.

4. The older ladies like to toss coins into the <u>soil / well</u>.

5. Some **words** in this **sentence** are <u>bowled / bold</u>.

6. It got colder, then we saw the snow <u>flurry / flurries</u>.

Exercise 32.6
Fill in the missing words, using the pictures as clues.

1. The lady is ___ ___ ___.

2. The doctor will ___ ___ ___ ___ the baby.

3. You put these on when it is ___ ___ ___ ___.

4. The coins were made of ___ ___ ___ ___.

5. The papers are in the ___ ___ ___ ___ ___ ___.

6. I like to put butter on my ___ ___ ___ ___.

Exercise 33.1

Circle the word that makes sense for each sentence below.

1 He sent a <u>necklace / message</u> that he would be late.

2. The strong boy had the <u>advantage / octopus</u>.

3. I received a <u>lampshade / package</u> in the mail.

4. We loaded our <u>baggage / toenails</u> into the van.

5. To play an instrument well, you must <u>service / practice</u>.

6. Will he <u>justice / notice</u> if we are late?

7. The performer danced on the <u>package / stage</u>.

8. Last year we had an <u>average / message</u> amount of rain.

Exercise 33.2
Write the **long vowel** sounds that are in the words.

1. kind		6. most	
2. right		7. child	
3. gold		8. mild	
4. roll		9. wild	
5. flight		10. post	

Exercise 33.3
Write the words below in their plural form.

1. story   _____

2. lady   _____

3. city   _____

4. delivery   _____

5. family   _____

6. factory   _____

Exercise 33.4
Circle the words that make sense for the sentences below.

1. In Florida <u>refrigerators / alligators</u> live in swamps.

2. We store our food in the <u>refrigerator / attic</u>.

3. At the <u>medical / amusement</u> park, we went on a roller-coaster.

4. A <u>compound / mythical</u> word is when two words are put together to make one word.

5. His story was not <u>convincing / hindering</u>.

Exercise 33.5
Review: change the words to their **past tense** forms.

1. plan _____   5. wake _____

2. take _____   6. eat _____

3. sell _____   7. go _____

4. run _____   8. hope _____

Exercise 34.1

Draw lines to match the contractions with their partners.

1.	I'm	I have
2.	I'll	have not
3.	I've	they have
4.	haven't	I am
5.	they're	they are
6.	they've	I will
7.	he's	did not
8.	didn't	he is
9.	doesn't	she is
10.	she's	does not

Exercise 34.2
Circle the contraction that makes sense.

1. <u>They're / They've</u> going to go to the grocery store later.

2. She <u>don't / doesn't</u> want to go home after class.

3. Do you think <u>she'll / she's</u> happy with her new pet?

4. <u>I've / I'm</u> going to go to the diner for dinner.

5. They <u>wasn't / weren't</u> going to stay for the weekend.

Exercise 34.3
Read the sentences and pick the two words that make sense and write the **contracted** form of those words on the line.

1. The baby _____*wouldn't*_____ eat the boiled chicken.
   would not   they are

2. I want to find out what _____ looking at.
   they are   did not

3. _____ been up all night with the kitten.
   Did not   We have

4. I _____ seen the car keys.
   did not   have not

5. You _____ talk in class.
   should not   they are

6. _____ going to go out later.
   We have   We are

Exercise 34.4
Complete the words with FLOSS words that make sense.

1. Dogs like to sn ___ ___ ___ other dogs.

2. To get service, you must ring the b ___ ___ ___ .

3. When fixing a cavity, the dentist may use a dr ___ ___ ___.

4. If you go away, I will m ___ ___ ___ you.

5. To do something perfectly requires a lot of sk ___ ___ ___.

6. The opposite of "more" is l ___ ___ ___ .

7. The child sp ___ ___ ___ ___ ___ his milk on the floor.

8. I had too much st ___ ___ ___ in my suitcase.

9. The boy would not swallow the p ___ ___ ___ .

10. If you eat too much, you will get f ___ ___ ___ .

Exercise 35.1
Circle the **homophone pairs** in the sentences below.
Note, there is **one** set of homophones in each sentence.

1. I won just one race at the picnic last summer.

2. The whole pool liner was replaced because of one hole.

3. I hear the music only when I'm here, next to the speaker.

4. The perfume that she sent to me had a nice scent.

5. In the morning, the maid made the bed.

6. The two girls ate too much ice-cream for dessert.

What word do you see in all of the homophones below?
Underline this word.

their   there   they're

their   **there**   **they're**
ownership   a place   "they are"

Exercise 35.2
Circle the correct homophone in the sentences below.

their   there   they're

1. Their / They're going to catch the morning train.

2. They carried their / there suitcases to the hotel room.

3. I kept their / there cell phones in my bag.

4. I wanted to go their / there , to the zoo, after lunch.

5. Their / There are three things you should do first.

6. Why are their / there no more shirts for sale?

7. I think there / they're waiting for it to rain first.

8. Their / There dog jumped up onto my lap.

9. I always wanted to go over there / they're.

10. What time do they get their / there dinner?

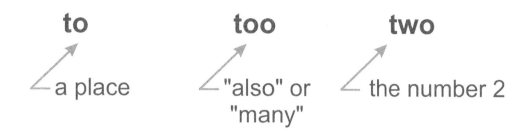

to → a place

too → "also" or "many"

two → the number 2

Exercise 35.3
Circle the correct homophone in the sentences below.

to   too   two

1. I wanted to / two / too go home after school.

2. I like that song to / two / too.

3. Jon had to / two / too many things to / two / too do.

4. On Saturday, the baby turned to / two / too years old.

5. Let's see who will go to / two / too the lake with us.

Exercise 35.4
Circle the words that complete the sentences.

1. In September, I will be in fourth / forth grade.

2. The bloodhound picked up the man's cent / scent.

3. She scent / sent the letter in the mail / male.

4. A girl is a female, and a boy is a mail / male.

5. Jon ran the race and one / won.

Exercise 35.5
Circle the correct word that corresponds to the given meaning.

1. When two things come together.	meet / meat
2. To purchase something.	bye / buy / by
3. Opposite of rich.	pore / poor / pour
4. Something you do with your eyes.	sea / see
5. Something you do with your ears.	here / hear
6. One penny is a __?__.	cent / sent
7. First, second, third, __?__.	forth / fourth
8. The past tense of "throw".	through / threw

Exercise 35.6
Review: write the contraction for the words below.

1. can not _____

2. do not _____

3. it is _____

4. she will _____

5. she is _____

Exercise 35.7
Add 'er' to the following words.

er

1. run _____

2. easy _____

3. cold _____

4. wet _____

5. happy _____

6. nice _____

7. fat _____

8. thin _____

Exercise 36.1
Circle the words that make sense in the sentences below.

1. The dog <u>whined / wind</u> when he wanted to go outside.

2. The car turned right as I moved the steering <u>wheel / well</u>.

3. It took a while, then his cry faded to a <u>whisper / whimper</u>.

4. In a library, you should talk in a soft <u>whine / whisper.</u>

5. The white <u>wheel / whale</u> can be found in the Artic.

Exercise 36.2
Circle the **silent letters** in the words below.

1. knee

2. knit

3. thumb

4. lamb

5. comb

6. knife

7. bomb

8. island

Exercise 36.3
Circle the word that matches the meaning.

1. The opposite of day.	knight / night
2. Use a pencil to do this.	write / right
3. Having to do with seeing.	sight / site
4. The opposite of "yes".	know / no
5. The opposite of "low"	high / hi
6. Sixty minutes.	hour / our
7. The past tense of "old".	knew / new
8. Means the entire thing.	whole / hole

Exercise 36.4
Circle the **silent letters** in the words below.

1. knight

2. two **2**

3. sword

4. autumn

5. wrong

6. write

Exercise 36.5
Fill in the missing letters for the words below.

1. g___ost	4. autum___	7. w___istle
2. w___ale	5. s___ord	8. ___rong
3. ___night	6. t___o **2**	9. ___rite

Exercise 36.6
Complete the words in the sentences below.

1. When you are very cold, your hands might get num____.

2. When you go to school, you learn to ____rite.

3. The coach blew his ___ ___ istle to start the race.

4. To open the door, turn the ____nob.

5. After summer comes autum____.

Exercise 37.1
Fill in the blanks to complete the words.

1.  ch__ __f

6.  d__ gg__ __

2. c__ __k__ __

7. __ __ght

3.  gen__ __

8. br__ __n__ __

4.  mov__ __

9.  b__ __t__ __

5.  hood__ __

10.  b__ __d__ __

Exercise 37.2
Read each sentence, and circle the words that make sense.

1. I don't <u>believe / belief</u> in ghosts.

2. It was a <u>relieve / relief</u> when I found my lost puppy.

3. The boys ran out onto the baseball <u>field / piece</u>.

4 Cut the cake into eight <u>cookies / pieces</u>.

5. Every morning the <u>freight / fight</u> train passes by.

6. The <u>brownie / genie</u> granted the man three wishes.

Exercise 37.3
Complete the sentences with the words that make sense.

brief   achieve   weight   neighbor   eight

1. I ate too much and gained _____.

2. The rain lasted for a _____ time.

3. When I was _____ years old, I was in third grade.

4. I would like to _____ my goals for today.

5. My _____ has a large pool.

Exercise 37.4

Read the words to your student, and have him/her circle the correct spelling for each word.

1.	free	frea	7.	brief	breaf
2.	seen	sean	8.	cooky	cookie
3.	feeld	field	9.	releef	relief
4.	eight	aight	10.	keep	keap
5.	fight	fite	11.	beleef	belief
6.	naybor	neighbor	12.	receeve	receive

Exercise 37.5

Write the sound that the underlined letter(s) make.

1.	right	long ____	5.	brief	long ____
2.	tray	long ____	6.	try	long ____
3.	high	long ____	7.	stray	long ____
4.	weigh	long ____	8.	series	long ____

Exercise 38.1

Complete the words below. Use 'ea' for the short 'e'

1.

m__ __sure

2.

tr__ __sure

3.

f__ __ __ __ers

4.

h__ __vy

5.

h__ __v__ __

6.

sw__ __t__ __

Exercise 38.2

Read the words out loud and draw lines to match the words to their pictures.

1. head

2. bread

3. weapon

4. wealthy

5. weather

6. heavy

7. heaven

8. thread

9. measure

10. sweater

Exercise 38.3
Complete the words below. Use 'ea' for the long 'a' sound.

1. p__ __ __

3. b__ __ __

2.  st__ __ __

4. 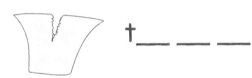 t__ __ __

Exercise 38.4
Read the sentences and circle the words that are correctly spelled.

1. Jane <u>said / sed</u> that I could go with her.

2. Jim leaned <u>agenst / against</u> the wall.

3. We planned on climbing the <u>mountain / mounten</u>.

4. We were <u>certen / certain</u> that he wasn't home.

5. I wish I could see you <u>agen / again</u> , before I go.

Exercise 38.5
Draw lines to match the rhyming words.

1. head		foam
2. eight		spite
3. limb		fine
4. sign		sealed
5. comb		him
6. right		leaf
7. field		bed
8. grief		state

Exercise 38.6
For each line below, circle the two words that rhyme.

1.	said	bread	paid
2.	seat	great	plate
3.	right	eight	late
4.	sweeter	sweater	wetter
5.	leather	leader	weather

Exercise 39.1
Circle the words that make sense for the sentences below.

1. It is <u>official / crucial</u> that you see a doctor.

2. My surprise birthday party was very <u>special / presidential</u>.

3. The document was marked <u>confidential / initial</u>.

4. We <u>initially / socially</u> wanted to leave early.

5. She had mud on her face for a <u>facial / financial</u>.

6. I live in a <u>residential / superficial</u> neighborhood.

Exercise 39.2
Circle the words that have the <u>long 'e'</u> sound (hint: there are 3).

tied	cookie	bear	eight
field	captain	great	movie

Exercise 39.3
Circle the sound for the letters that are underlined.

1. br<u>ie</u>f   long 'e'   long 'i'
2. f<u>ie</u>ld   long 'e'   long 'i'
3. br<u>ea</u>th   long 'e'   short 'e'
4. br<u>ea</u>the   long 'e'   short 'e'
5. beh<u>i</u>nd   long 'i'   short 'i'
6. s<u>ai</u>d   long 'a'   short 'e'
7. <u>gr</u>e<u>a</u>t   long 'a'   long 'e'
8. cert<u>ai</u>n   long 'a'   short 'e'

Exercise 39.4
Draw lines to match the rhyming words.

1. climb   gum

2. numb   bite

3. known   spout

4. which   led

5. tight   pitch

6. head   chime

7. doubt   groan

Exercise 39.5
Complete the crossword puzzle.

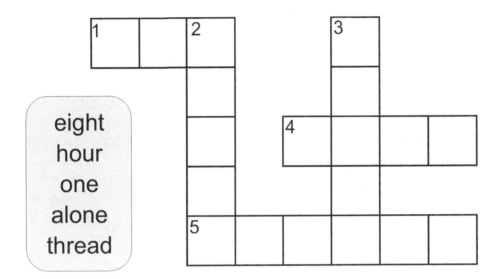

eight
hour
one
alone
thread

Across

1. The number before two.

4. Sixty minutes makes an___.

5. To sew, you need a needle and ___.

Down

2. The number that comes before nine.

3. When you are all by yourself, you are ___.

Exercise 40.1
Draw lines to match the words to their correct math equation.

1. addition $3 \times 4 = 12$

2. subtraction $2 + 1 = 3$

3. multiplication $8 \div 4 = 2$

4. division $5 - 4 = 1$

Exercise 40.2
Complete the sentences with the words that make sense.

| lotion | mission | caution | transportation | solution |

1. The team of astronauts were on a _____ to land on the moon.

2. People use _____ on their dry skin.

3. Planes, trains and automobiles are forms of _____.

4. Our teacher wanted to know the _____ to the problem.

5. You must use _____ when walking on ice.

Exercise 40.3
Circle the sound that the <u>underlined</u> letters make.

1. gr<u>ea</u>t	long 'e'	long 'a'
2. m<u>igh</u>t	long 'i'	long 'a'
3. w<u>ei</u>ght	long 'e'	long 'a'
4. <u>ei</u>ght	long 'e'	long 'a'
5. br<u>ie</u>f	long 'e'	long 'i'
6. f<u>ie</u>ld	long 'e'	long 'i'

Exercise 40.4
Read the sentences and circle the correct words.

1. To find the meaning of a word, you use a ?.

mission   dictionary

2. The number of people that live in a certain place.

creation   population

3. A person who is an expert in his or her work.

professional   tension

4. The meaning of a certain word.

passion   definition

5. A connection that a person has to another person.

nation   relationship

Exercise 40.5
Circle the words that makes sense for the sentences below.

1. The old car was in good condition / transition.

2. My special catcher's mitt was swimming / missing.

3. The dancer went to submission / audition for the show.

4. Believe it or not, he was telling the truth / bathtub.

5. We play soccer on a pillow / field.

6. He likes to eat bread / kittens with peanut butter.

Exercise 40.6
Circle the words that makes sense for the sentences below. Be careful, the words are homophones, and you may need help.

1. I need a new <u>pair / pear</u> of sneakers.

2. I like bananas, apples, and <u>pairs / pears</u>.

3. For dinner, I will order <u>stake / steak</u>.

4. We use a <u>stake / steak</u> to fix the tent to the ground.

5. Please <u>grate / great</u> the cheese for the salad.

6. You did a <u>great / grate</u> job on your project.

Exercise 40.7
Circle the sound that the <u>underlined</u> letters make.

1.	f<u>igh</u>t	long 'i'	long 'a'
2.	r<u>ea</u>dy	long 'e'	short 'e'
3.	inst<u>ea</u>d	long 'e'	short 'e'
4.	rel<u>ie</u>f	long 'e'	long 'i'
5.	n<u>ei</u>ghbor	long 'e'	long 'a'

Exercise R4.1

Circle the words that are correctly spelled.

1. answer   anser   5.   rong   wrong

2.   dout   doubt   6.   clime   climb

3.   thum   thumb   7.   island   iland

4.   toward   toard   8.   crum   crumb

Exercise R4.2

Write the **plural** form of the words below.

1. batch   _____

2. wish   _____

3. box   _____

4. city   _____

5. knife   _____

Exercise R4.3

Complete the sentences below with the words that make sense.

knot   knife   knee   answer   knob   know

1. Your leg bends at the _____ .

2. What is the _____ to the question?

3. It is nice to _____ a lot about a subject.

4. To cut the meat you'll need a _____ .

5. His shoe laces were tied in a _____ .

6. Turn the door- _____ to open the door.

Exercise R4.4
Circle the words that are correctly spelled.

1. ate / eight

2. cookie / cooky

3. bread / bred

4. pair / pear

5. swetter / sweater

6. head / hed

7. bear / bair

8. welthy / wealthy

Exercise R4.5
Complete the sentences below with the words that make sense.

> healthy   vision   nutrition   measure   wealthy

1. Bad eye-sight means poor _____ .

2. You may use a ruler to _____ something.

3. If you're not sick, then you are _____ .

4. If you have a lot of money, you are _____ .

5. You must eat proper food for good _____ .

Exercise R4.6
Draw lines to match the words to their contractions.

1.	I will	they'll
2.	I am	we've
3.	they are	I'll
4.	they will	it'll
5.	it is	they're
6.	it will	it's
7.	we have	we're
8.	we are	I'm

Exercise R4.7
Circle the **five** words where **'ea'** has the **short 'e'** sound.

meat heat bear health

head feather dear beach

great heavy ready real

Exercise 41.1
Circle the words that have apostrophes for ownership.

   * Be careful, not all apostrophes are for ownership!

1. I doubt my grandfather's vision is good.

2. The baby's crib is purple.

3. They're looking at Jim's new bicycle.

4. It's interesting how the bird's feathers are so bright.

5. My father's car was in a collision.

6. Where did you go with Sam's bicycle?

7. We're going to go to Emily's house.

8. The dogs' dishes were empty.

Exercise 41.2
Add apostrophes for ownership; some words may need an apostrophe and some may not.

1. My <u>dogs</u> hair is brown.

2. My three <u>dogs</u> all like to eat meat.

3. <u>Johns</u> house is just around the corner.

4. The teacher collected the <u>students</u> papers.

5. <u>Jills</u> bicycle was leaning against the house.

Exercise 41.3
Circle the correct words for the sentences below.

1. She likes the fact that <u>its / it's</u> Friday.

2. After lunch, <u>their / they're</u> going to the library.

3. We <u>were / we're</u> looking for a nice place for our vacation.

4. What do you think of <u>there / their</u> new puppy?

5. What is Frank going to do when he gets <u>there / their</u> ?

6. <u>Were / We're</u> you at the store earlier today?

Exercise 41.4
Circle the sounds on the right that match the sounds on the left. There is one match per line.

1. tion	igh	sion	tial
2. oy	oo	ou	oi
3. ew	oi	oo	ou
4. cial	tial	tion	ew
5. oa	ew	au	ow
6. ee	ea	ew	ai
7. ai	oi	ay	ie
8. ie	igh	ow	ue
9. er	or	ar	ur
10. aw	er	au	ow

Exercise 41.5
Complete the words in the sentences below.

1. On the boat, I got m_o_ _t_ _i_ _o_ _n_ sickness.

2. I tried to answer the ques___ ___ ___ ___.

3. There was a big birthday celebr___ ___ ___ ___ ___.

4. I had to find the defin___ ___ ___ ___ ___ for the word.

5. She went to the hospital for an oper___ ___ ___ ___ ___.

Exercise 41.6
Write the words, with apostrophes for ownership, on the lines.

1. _____ puppy was very excited to see me.
          Jade

2. _____ turtle likes to watch television.
          Amy

3. The girls went to _____ house after school.
               Joey

4. I borrowed _____ pencil.
            Mary

5. My _____ classroom was decorated nicely.
        teacher

6. The _____ bathroom is down the hallway.
      boys (more than one)

Exercise 41.7
Circle the **four** words that have the **long 'a'** sound.

weight	raining	tank
mountain	again	fountain
curtain	braid	bargain

Exercise 42.1

Circle the sounds on the right that match the <u>underlined</u> letters on the left.

1. potat<u>o</u>	long 'o'	/uh/	'e'-'o'
2. extr<u>a</u>	long 'o'	/uh/	'e'-'o'
3. rad<u>io</u>	long 'o'	/uh/	'e'-'o'
4. stud<u>io</u>	long 'o'	/uh/	'e'-'o'
5. zebr<u>a</u>	long 'o'	/uh/	'e'-'o'
6. zer<u>o</u>	long 'o'	/uh/	'e'-'o'
7. als<u>o</u>	long 'o'	/uh/	'e'-'o'
8. dat<u>a</u>	long 'o'	/uh/	'e'-'o'

Exercise 42.2

Complete the sentences with the words that make sense.

family   America   tornado   bacteria   tomato

1. Seek shelter if a _____ is near.

2. An infection can be caused by a _____.

3. I planted _____ plants in my garden.

4. The large _____ needs a mini-van.

5. The president of _____ can veto a bill.

Exercise 42.3
Circle the words that make sense for the sentences below.

1. For lunch we'll have <u>tuna / tuba</u> fish sandwiches.

2. Let's take a ride in the <u>pasta / taxi</u>.

3. Last winter it got below <u>zero / mini</u> degrees.

4. We listened to the music on the <u>pizza / radio</u>.

5. Put your feet up on the <u>sofa / piano</u> and relax!

6. Use a <u>comma / coma</u> to separate words in a list.

7. Our teacher gave us <u>soda / extra</u> homework.

Exercise 42.4
Complete the words for the pictures below.

1. z _ _ _ _

5. t _ _ _ _

2. _ _ z z _

6. p _ _ _ _

3. t _ _ _

7. p _ _ _ _ _

4. r _ _ _ _

8. t _ _ _ _ _

Exercise 42.5
Circle the words that make sense in the sentences below.

1. The <u>sodium / helium</u> balloon floated into the air.

2. The boy would not eat the <u>ingredient / broccoli.</u>

3. A sentence usually ends with a <u>librarian / period</u>.

4. Jim ordered a <u>medium / helium</u> sized soda.

5. I have a lot of <u>experience / material</u> in gymnastics.

6. I needed to purchase a <u>stadium / medium</u> sized shirt.

7. She wouldn't reveal her secret <u>ingredient / librarian</u>.

8. He stuffed the tomato and lettuce into the <u>patio / pita</u>.

9. We went to the <u>stadium / broccoli</u> to see the game.

10. A person who studies history is a <u>historian / hysterical</u>.

Exercise 43.1
Complete the words below; all words end with 'le'.

1. c _ _ _ _

3. a _ _ _ _

2. h _ _ _ _ _

4. t _ _ _ _ _

Exercise 43.2
Complete the words below.

Remember to protect your short vowels.

1. k _ _ _ _ _

4. b _ _ _ _ _

2. a _ _ _ _

5. b _ _ _ _ _

3. p _ _ _ _ _

6. w _ _ _ _ _

Exercise 43.3
Circle the words that make sense in the sentences below.

1. He was not able to jump over the riddle / puddle.

2. The rotten apple / puzzle was not edible.

3. The baby wanted the kettle / bottle of milk.

4. Hold the pitcher by its middle / handle.

5. The puppy likes to cuddle / battle with the boy.

6. The horrible disease was not invisible / curable.

7. The gymnast was very flexible / notable.

Exercise 43.4
Complete the sentences with the words that make sense.

> visible   ankle   stable   possible   noodles

1. Cook the _____ in boiling water.

2. The horse stays in the _____ .

3. At nighttime, the sun is not _____ .

4. The skater tripped and broke her _____ .

5. It is not _____ to touch your elbow to your chin.

Exercise 43.5
Write the sound that the underlined letter(s) make.

1. bel<u>ie</u>ve   long ___

2. gr<u>ea</u>t   long ___

3. fl<u>igh</u>t   long ___

4. b<u>ea</u>r   long ___

5. moun<u>ai</u>n   short ___

6. br<u>ea</u>d   short ___

7. capt<u>ai</u>n   short ___

8. pos<u>i</u>tion   short ___

Exercise 44.1
Circle the words that make sense in the sentences below.

1. The picture hung on the wall in the hallway / pool.

2. Put your signature on the bottom of the shark / paper.

3. Can a crystal ball be used to see the future / tornado?

4. On nature walks, one can see many lampshades / birds.

5. We played Capture the Flag in gym / potato class.

6. Stand up straight for good structure / posture.

7. The trip was quite an adventure / expenditure.

Exercise 44.2

Circle the sounds on the right that match the sounds on the left. There is only one per line.

1. ture	/shun/	/chur/	long 'u'
2. tion	/shur/	/shun/	/chur/
3. sure	/shull/	/shun/	/shur/
4. igh	long 'a'	long 'i'	/j/
5. ay	long 'a'	/ou/	long'e'
6. tial	/shun/	long 'i'	/shull/
7. cial	/shun/	long 'i'	/shull/
8. sion	/shun/	/oy/	/shur/

Exercise 44.3
Circle the words that make sense in the sentences below.

1. A <u>mixture / pressure</u> of sugar water can make candy.

2. The sheep were out in the <u>picture / pasture</u>.

3. The <u>texture / temperature</u> is ninety degrees.

4. The boy fell and <u>fractured / measured</u> his arm.

5. Tom <u>measured / punctured</u> the balloon with a needle.

6. In the <u>nature / future</u> , you should check the weather.

Exercise 44.4
Circle the answers to the questions below.

1. When 'c' is followed by 'e', 'i', or 'y', it <u>always / sometimes</u> has the /s/ sound.

2. When 'g' is followed by 'e', 'i', or 'y', it <u>always / sometimes</u> has the /j/ sound.

3. Often, an 'i' can have the <u>long 'a' / long 'e'</u> sound.

4. When 'y' is in the **middle** of a word, it can have the long or short <u>'e' sound / 'i' sound</u>.

5. Can a word **end** with the letter 'j'? <u>yes / no</u>

Exercise 44.5

Write the words below in their **plural** form.

1. story _____

2. lady _____

3. party _____

4. baby _____

5. * ability _____

6. * body _____

7. memory _____

8. dictionary _____

Words Ending with 'ous' and 'ious'

Exercise 45.1
Circle the words that make sense in the sentences below.

1. If you are very well known, you are <u>famous / serious</u>.

2. When studying, you should be <u>nervous / serious</u>.

3. If someone is very pretty, they are <u>famous / gorgeous</u>.

4. Monkeys are often described as <u>glamorous / curious</u>.

5. Walking in the middle of the road is <u>dangerous / famous</u>.

Exercise 45.2
Circle the words that make sense in the sentences below.

1. The <u>precious / nutritious</u> gem stone sparkled.

2. The meal was very <u>nutritious / suspicious</u>.

3. The police officer said the boy was <u>suspicious / precious</u>.

4. Be <u>cautious / dangerous</u> when walking on ice.

5. People who worry a lot may be <u>suspicious / anxious</u>.

6. The <u>gracious / vicious</u> lie was spread around the town.

7. The host of the party was very <u>gracious / obnoxious</u>.

8. My little brother thinks he's funny, but he is really <u>anxious / obnoxious</u>

Exercise 45.3
Circle the sounds on the right that match the underlined letters on the left.

1. fam<u>ous</u>	/us/	/shus/	'e' - /us/
2. obv<u>ious</u>	/us/	/shus/	'e' - /us/
3. nerv<u>ous</u>	/us/	/shus/	'e' - /us/
4. gra<u>cious</u>	/us/	/shus/	'e' - /us/
5. cau<u>tious</u>	/us/	/shus/	'e' - /us/
6. danger<u>ous</u>	/us/	/shus/	'e' - /us/
7. ser<u>ious</u>	/us/	/shus/	'e' - /us/
8. suspi<u>cious</u>	/us/	/shus/	'e' - /us/

Exercise 45.4
Circle the words that make sense in the sentences.

1. If you are very angry, you are <u>glamorous / furious</u>.

2. The dancer practiced in the <u>studio / radio</u>.

3. The popular boy has <u>numerous / obvious</u> friends.

4. <u>Too / Two</u> and "also" mean the same thing.

5. The answer to the problem is <u>obvious / dangerous</u>.

Exercise 45.5
Circle the matching sounds, there is one per line.

1. ous	us	ou	oy
2. oi	'o'	oy	ou
3. tial	tale	shull	tile
4. tion	tial	cial	shun
5. cial	shull	us	shun
6. eigh	'a'	'e'	'i'
7. igh	'a'	'e'	'i'

Exercise 45.6
Add 'ing' to the following words and read them out loud.

ing

1. run   _____

2. slip   _____

3. carry   _____

4. identify   _____

5. shake   _____

6. break   _____

Exercise 45.7

Circle the meanings to the definitions listed.

1. Acting more than your age: <u>mature / nutritious</u>

2. The same: <u>capture / equal</u>

3. Tastes great: <u>delicious / solution</u>

4. Feeling sorry for: <u>division / compassion</u>

5. A very large house: <u>mansion / envious</u>

6. A different form of something: <u>version / alter</u>

7. Easy to see: <u>curious / obvious</u>

8. Many or a lot of: <u>nervous / numerous</u>

9. Harmful: <u>dangerous / suspicious</u>

10. To be extra careful: <u>cautious / anxious</u>

Exercise 46.1
Circle the words that make sense in the sentences below.

1. The gold handbag was very <u>expensive / abusive</u>.

2. The opposite of positive is <u>inventive / negative</u>.

3. Her package will <u>survive / arrive</u> next Friday.

4. The boys were very <u>talkative / expensive</u>.

5. The movie star was very <u>relative / attractive</u>.

6. The artist is very <u>creative / aggressive</u>.

7. His puppies are very <u>negative / active</u>.

8. The holiday party is very <u>assertive / festive</u>.

Exercise 46.2
Circle the sounds that the underlined 'i's makes.

1.	str<u>i</u>ve	long 'i'	short 'i'
2.	dr<u>i</u>ve	long 'i'	short 'i'
3.	g<u>i</u>ve	long 'i'	short 'i'
4.	fest<u>i</u>ve	long 'i'	short 'i'
5.	surv<u>i</u>ve	long 'i'	short 'i'
6.	al<u>i</u>ve	long 'i'	short 'i'

Exercise 46.3
Answer the questions below.

1. For words that end with /v/, use ___ ___ for the /v/.

2. For words that end with /j/, use: ___ ___ for the /j/.

3. What letters after 'c' turns 'c' into /s/? ___ ___ ___

4. What letters after 'g' can turn 'g' into /j/? ___ ___ ___

Exercise 46.4
Write the words for the pictures below.

1. _ _ _ _ _   _ _ _ _ _ _

2. _ _ _ _   _ _ _ _ _ _

3. _ _ _ _ _   _ _ _ _ _ _ _

4. _ _ _ _   _ _ _ _ _ _

Exercise 46.5
Circle the words that make sense in the sentences below.

1. We rearranged the <u>furnace / furniture</u> in Justin's room.

2. I used <u>solution / lotion</u> on my dry hands.

3. Driving in a snow storm is <u>cautious / dangerous</u>.

4. The baby was a nice <u>condition / addition</u> to the family.

5. The <u>initial / special</u> delivery arrived yesterday morning.

Exercise 47.1
Draw lines to match the words to their pictures.

1. para<u>ch</u>ute

2. <u>ch</u>andelier

3. ma<u>ch</u>ine

4. <u>ch</u>ef

5. stoma<u>ch</u>

6. <u>ch</u>emicals

7. musta<u>ch</u>e

8. <u>ch</u>ivalry

9. s<u>ch</u>ool

10. me<u>ch</u>anic

Exercise 47.2
Circle the words where 'ch' has the /k/ sound (there are 5).

ch = /k/

para<u>ch</u>ute   me<u>ch</u>anic   a<u>ch</u>e   <u>ch</u>aos

e<u>ch</u>o   s<u>ch</u>ool   <u>ch</u>arm   <u>ch</u>ampion

Exercise 47.3
Circle the words that make sense in the sentences below.

1. When I'm hungry, my <u>stomach / machine</u> may growl.

2. I woke up with a bad head- <u>echo / ache</u>.

3. The <u>mechanic / character</u> in the story was brave.

4. What <u>chemicals / parachutes</u> do they use to clean?

5. The hotel lobby had a large <u>parachute / chandelier</u>.

Exercise 47.4
Circle sound that the 'ch' makes in the words below.

1.	e<u>ch</u>o	/ch/ as in "chop"	/k/	/sh/
2.	s<u>ch</u>ool	/ch/ as in "chop"	/k/	/sh/
3.	<u>ch</u>ef	/ch/ as in "chop"	/k/	/sh/
4.	<u>ch</u>annel	/ch/ as in "chop"	/k/	/sh/
5.	<u>ch</u>emist	/ch/ as in "chop"	/k/	/sh/
6.	<u>Ch</u>icago	/ch/ as in "chop"	/k/	/sh/
7.	wren<u>ch</u>	/ch/ as in "chop"	/k/	/sh/
8.	Mi<u>ch</u>igan	/ch/ as in "chop"	/k/	/sh/
9.	<u>ch</u>ord	/ch/ as in "chop"	/k/	/sh/
10.	me<u>ch</u>anic	/ch/ as in "chop"	/k/	/sh/

Exercise 47.5

For each sentence, complete the missing words with the sounds listed.

| ture | ation | tion | ive | ous | ach | atch | igh |

1. F i c _ _ _ _ _ _ means that the story isn't real.

2. The f a m _ _ _ actor stopped to pose for pictures.

3. We go to school to get an e d u c _ _ _ _ _ _.

4. If hungry, your s t o m _ _ _ may growl.

5. The dog used his leg to s c r _ _ _ _ his itch.

6. The sun was too b r _ _ _ _ t to look at.

7. I took a p i c _ _ _ _ _ of my best friend.

8. To stay healthy, you should keep a c t _ _ _ _.

Exercise 48.1
Circle the words that make sense in the sentences below.

1. The <u>dolphin / phone</u> rang three times.

2. The globe has the shape of a <u>elephant / sphere</u>.

3. We saw the <u>orphan / dolphin</u> jump out of the water.

4. If you are in first place you may get a <u>graphic / trophy</u>.

5. The man on stage spoke into a <u>microphone / phantom</u>.

6. There are twenty-six letters in the <u>trophy / alphabet</u>.

Exercise 48.2
Complete the sentences with the words that make sense.

> rough   cough   laugh   enough   tough   graph

1. We had _____ cake to share with everyone.

2. In science class, we had to plot a _____ .

3. Sandpaper is not soft, it is very _____ .

4. The science test wasn't easy, it was _____ .

5. When Ethan got sick, he had a bad _____ .

6. The funny joke made me _____ .

Exercise 48.3
Complete the words using the given letters.

b   br   th   f

1. The two angry boys ____ought over the toy truck.

2. She ____ought she knew the answer.

3. I went to the store and __ought a new dress.

4. He __ought his little brother over to our house.

Exercise 48.4
Circle the words that make sense in the sentences below.

1. The lady's daughter came home from mars / school.

2. We were taught how to add and subtract / drive.

3. The past tense of "think" is thunk / thought.

4. Grandma bought / fought a new outfit at the store.

5. Ryan brought / bought his favorite movie to the party.

Exercise 48.5
Match the sounds below.

1. ph		/chur/
2. igh		/shur/
3. aught		/v/
4. sure		long 'i'
5. oi		/j/
6. ous		oy
7. ture		/us/
8. ve		/awt/
9. ge		/s/
10. ce		/f/

Exercise 49.1

Draw lines to match the words to their pictures.

1. musician

2. electrician

3. physician

4. beautician

5. magician

6. mathematician

7. politician

8. optician

Exercise 49.2
Complete the sentences with the words that make sense.

nutritious	musician	daughter	electrician
style	famous	imitation	poisonous

1. The _____ magician was at the show.

2. The _____ came to fix the light switch.

3. The fake diamond was a poor _____.

4. Watch out for the _____ snake!

5. The dietician will create a _____ meal.

6. I went to the beautician to get a new hair _____.

7. The _____ played the violin.

8. She taught her _____ how to swim.

Exercise 49.3
Circle the sound for the letters that are underlined.

1. <u>ph</u>obia   /f/   /p/

2. <u>ch</u>ef   /k/   /sh/

3. me<u>ch</u>anic   /k/   /sh/

4. pic<u>ture</u>   /tor/   /chur/

5. danger<u>ous</u>   /shus/   /us/

Exercise 49.4

Circle the sound for the letter(s) that are underlined.

1. m<u>i</u>nd	long 'e'	long 'i'
2. <u>ei</u>ght	long 'e'	long 'a'
3. phob<u>ia</u>	long 'e'	long 'i'
4. s<u>igh</u>	long 'i'	short 'e'
5. h<u>ea</u>lth	long 'e'	short 'e'
6. r<u>ea</u>dy	long 'e'	short 'e'
7. gr<u>ea</u>t	long 'e'	long 'a'
8. hell<u>o</u>	short 'o'	long 'o'

Exercise 49.5

Write the past tense form of the words below. Use the sentence: "Today I ___, but yesterday I ___."

<u>aught / ought</u>

1. teach _____

2. fight _____

3. catch _____

4. think _____

5. buy _____

Exercise 50.1
Write the un-contracted words on the lines below.

1. couldn't   _____

2. didn't   _____

3. that's   _____

4. they've   _____

5. weren't   _____

6. you've   _____

Exercise 50.2
Circle the words where 'et' has the long 'a' sound (there are 6).

fillet	basket	ratchet
quiet	crochet	gourmet
ballet	bouquet	valet

Exercise 50.3
Circle five the words where 'ea' has the short 'e' sound.

dr<u>ea</u>m   l<u>ea</u>ther   l<u>ea</u>f

p<u>ea</u>k   ch<u>ea</u>t   br<u>ea</u>d

d<u>ea</u>f   w<u>ea</u>ther   spr<u>ea</u>d

Exercise 50.4
Circle the correct word for each sentence. Be careful, these are homophones, and you may not know which one to use.

1. The strong boy lifted the <u>weight / wait</u> over his head.

2. The wind <u>blue / blew</u> the door open.

3. The <u>some / sum</u> of one plus one is two.

4. The girl dressed up as a <u>which / witch</u> for Halloween.

5. The young couple drove down the <u>rode / road</u>.

6. The group <u>new / knew</u> how to find the train station.

Exercise 50.5
Circle the words that have the /f/ sound for the underlined letters (there are 6).

bou<u>gh</u>t   enou<u>gh</u>   dau<u>gh</u>ter   cou<u>gh</u>   tou<u>gh</u>

rou<u>gh</u>   <u>ph</u>ony   lau<u>gh</u>   cau<u>gh</u>t   brou<u>gh</u>t

Exercise 50.6
Circle the correct word(s) for each sentence.

1. The little boy drew on the <u>piece / peace</u> of paper.

2. The <u>pore / poor</u> man begged for some money.

3. Don't <u>waste / waist</u> the expensive steak.

4. The money was <u>due / do / dew</u> at the meeting.

5. The boy <u>rights / writes</u> with his <u>right / write</u> hand.

6. The play-set is <u>made / maid</u> of <u>wood / would</u>.

7. I <u>herd / heard</u> that you ate the <u>whole / hole</u> pie!

8. The <u>sun / son</u> was <u>hi / high</u> in the sky.

Exercise 50.7
Circle the words where the 'h' is silent (there are 3).

<u>h</u>ip   <u>h</u>onor   <u>h</u>ockey

<u>h</u>ello   <u>h</u>amburger   <u>h</u>istory

<u>h</u>our   <u>h</u>orrible   <u>h</u>onest

Exercise R5.1
Add apostrophes for ownership to the missing words.

1. _____ joke made me laugh!
   Jane

2. _____ turtle was caught trying to escape.
   Amy

3. The _____ cage needed to be cleaned.
   gerbils (more than one)

4. A rabbit was hiding in the _____ hat.
   magician

5. The_____ room needed to be cleaned.
   sisters (more than one)

Exercise R5.2
Circle the sound that the underlined letter(s) make.

1.	bacter<u>ia</u>	long 'i'	'e' - /uh/
2.	rad<u>io</u>	long 'i'	'e' - 'o'
3.	tax<u>i</u>	long 'e'	long 'i'
4.	stud<u>io</u>	long 'i'	'e' - 'o'
5.	Americ<u>a</u>	/uh/	long 'a'
6.	Chicag<u>o</u>	/oo/	long 'o'
7.	Alask<u>a</u>	/uh/	long 'a'

Exercise R5.3

Circle the words that complete the sentences.

1. The magician through / threw knives at his assistant.

2. The vulture flew / flu out of it's / its nest.

3. The angry boy went an hour / our without talking.

4. The ballet dancer wore a tutu around her waist / waste.

5. The chef made / maid a fish fillet dinner.

6. The famous actor passed / past by us without stopping.

7. The technician new / knew how to fix the radio.

Exercise R5.4
Unscramble the letters to complete the words.

1.

g u
a h

l__ __ __ __

2.

abcdefg
hijklmnop
qrstuv
wxyz

h p
a

al__ __ __ bet

3.

u o
g h

c__ __ __ __ syrup

4.

h y
p o

tr__ __ __ __

5.

h p
o
e n

micro__ __ __ __ __

6.

a p
r
g h

bar__ __ __ __ __

7.

i p
h n

dol__ __ __ __

8.

h p
a
t n

ele__ __ __ __ __

Exercise R5.5
Complete the sentences with the words that make sense.

culture   pasture   temperature   curious   mixture

1. The _____ cat opened the lid to investigate.

2. The drink is a _____ of soda and fruit juice.

3. The cows grazed out in the _____.

4. If you visit another country, you'll see their _____.

5. A thermometer tells you the current _____.

Exercise R5.6
Read each word out loud, and circle the sound that the underlined letters make.

1.	plea<u>se</u>	/z/	/s/
2.	relea<u>se</u>	/z/	/s/
3.	nerv<u>ous</u>	/us/	/s/
4.	lo<u>se</u>	/z/	/s/
5.	loo<u>se</u>	/z/	/s/
6.	me<u>ch</u>anic	/k/	/sh/
7.	ball<u>et</u>	long 'i'	long 'a'

Made in the USA
Monee, IL
04 November 2022

17034854R00103